ICEBOUND

By Owen Davis

THE DETOUR
ICEBOUND

ICEBOUND
A Play

BY

OWEN DAVIS

BOSTON

LITTLE, BROWN, AND COMPANY

1923

FOREWORD

With the production of "The Detour," about a year ago, I managed to secure some measure of success in drawing a simple picture of life as it is lived on a Long Island farm; encouraged by this, I am now turning toward my own people, the people of northern New England, whose folklore, up to the present time, has been quite neglected in our theatre. I mean, of course, that few serious attempts have been made in the direction of a genre comedy of this locality. Here I have at least tried to draw a true picture of these people, and I am of their blood, born of generations of Northern Maine, small-town folk, and brought up among them. In my memory of them is little of the "Rube" caricature of the conventional theatre; they are neither buffoons nor sentimentalists, and at least neither their faults nor their virtues are borrowed from the melting pot but are the direct result of their own heritage and environment.

OWEN DAVIS.

1923.

ICEBOUND

"Icebound" was originally produced in New York, February 10, 1923, with the following cast:

HENRY JORDAN.........................*John Westley*
EMMA, his wife.......................*Lotta Linthicum*
NETTIE, her daughter by a former marriage.*Boots Wooster*
SADIE FELLOWS, once Sadie Jordan, a widow..*Eva Condon*
ORIN, her son....................*Andrew J. Lawlor, Jr.*
ELLA JORDAN, the unmarried sister.......*Frances Neilson*
DOCTOR CURTIS....................*Lawrence Eddinger*
JANE CROSBY, a second cousin of the Jordans.*Phyllis Povah*
JUDGE BRADFORD....................*Willard Robertson*
BEN JORDAN............................*Robert Ames*
HANNAH............................*Edna May Oliver*
JIM JAY............................*Charles Henderson*

ACT ONE.

THE PARLOR OF THE JORDAN HOMESTEAD, 4 P.M., October, 1922.

ACT TWO.

THE SITTING ROOM OF THE JORDAN HOMESTEAD, Two months later. Afternoon.

ACT THREE.

SAME AS ACT I, Late in the following March.

ICEBOUND

ACT ONE

Scene: The parlor of the Jordan Homestead at Venzie, Maine.

It is late October, and through the two windows at the back one may see a bleak countryside, the grass brown and lifeless, and the bare limbs of the trees silhouetted against a gray sky. Here, in the room that for a hundred years has been the rallying point of the Jordan family, a group of relatives are gathered to await the death of the old woman who is the head of their clan. The room in which they wait is as dull and as drab as the lives of those who have lived within its walls. Here we have the cleanliness that is next to godliness, but no sign of either comfort or beauty, both of which are looked upon with suspicion as being sign-posts on the road to perdition.

In this group are the following characters: Henry Jordan, a heavy set man of fifty, worn by his business cares into a dull sort of hopeless resignation. Emma, his wife, a stout and rather formidable woman of forty, with a look of chronic displeasure; Nettie, her daughter by a former marriage, a vain and shallow little rustic beauty; Sadie, a thin, tight-lipped woman of forty, a widow and a gossip; Orin, her son, a pasty-faced boy of ten with large spectacles; Ella, a "Maiden lady" of thirty-six, restless and dissatisfied.

Ella and Sadie, true Jordans by birth, are a degree above Emma in social standing, at least they were until Henry's marriage to Emma made her a somewhat resentful member of the family. In Emma's dialogue and in her reactions, I have attempted a rather nice distinction between the two grades of rural middle-class folk; the younger characters here, as in most other communities, have advanced one step.

Rise: At rise there is a long silence; the occupants of the room are ill at ease. Emma is grim and frowning. Nettie sits with a simper of youthful vanity, looking stealthily at herself from time to time in a small mirror set in the top of her cheap vanity case. Ella and Sadie have been crying and dab at their eyes a bit ostentatiously. Henry makes a thoughtful note with a pencil, then returns his notebook to his pocket and warms his hands at the stove.

There is a low whistle of a cold autumn wind as some dead leaves are blown past the window. Orin, who has a cold in his head, sniffs viciously; the others, with the exception of his mother, look at him in remonstrance. An eight-day clock in sight, through the door to the hall, strikes four.

EMMA (*sternly*)
    Four o'clock.
HENRY (*looks at watch*)
    Five minutes of. That clock's been fast for more 'n thirty years.
NETTIE (*looks at wrist watch*)
    My watch says two minutes after.

HENRY

Well, it's wrong!

EMMA (*acidly*)

You gave it to her yourself, did n't you?

SADIE (*sighs*)

Good Land! What does it matter?

NETTIE (*offended*)

Oh! Does n't it? Oh!

ELLA

Maybe it does to you. She ain't your blood relation.

EMMA

Nettie loves her grandma, don't you dear?

NETTIE

Some folks not so far off may get fooled before long about how much grandma and I was to each other.

EMMA (*sternly*)

You hush!

[*Again there is a pause, and again it is broken by a loud sniff from Orin, as the women look at him in disgust. Sadie speaks up in his defense.*

SADIE

He's got kind of a cold in his head.

HENRY

The question is, ain't he got a handkerchief?

SADIE

Here, Orin!

[*She hands him her handkerchief.*

ELLA

The idea! No handkerchief when you 've come expectin' some one to die!

ORIN

I had one, but I used it up.

[*He blows his nose.*

HENRY

After four.   Well, I expect they 'll have to close the store without me.

ELLA

I left everything just as soon as Jane sent me word!

SADIE

Why should Jane be with her instead of you or me, her own daughters?

HENRY

You girls always made her nervous, and I guess she 's pretty low.   (*He looks at his watch again*)   I said I'd be back before closin' time.   I don't know as I dare to trust those boys.

EMMA

You can't tell about things, when Sadie's husband died we sat there most all night.

SADIE (*angrily*)

Yes, and you grudged it to him, I knew it then and it is n't likely I 'm going to forget it.

ELLA

Will was a good man, but even you can't say he was ever very dependable.

EMMA

My first husband died sudden — (*she turns to Nettie*) — you can't remember it, dear.

ELLA

You did n't remember it very long, it wa'n't much more'n a year before you married Henry.

HENRY (*sighs*)

Well, he was as dead then as he 's ever got to be. (*He turns and glances nervously out window*)   I don't know but what I could just run down to the store for a minute, then hurry right back.

SADIE

You 're the oldest of her children, a body would think you 'd be ashamed.

HENRY

Oh, I 'll stay.

[*There is a silence. Orin sniffs. Ella glares at him.*

ELLA

Of course he *could* sit somewheres else.

[*Sadie puts her arm about Orin and looks spitefully at Ella. Doctor Curtis, an elderly country physician, comes down the stairs and enters the room, all turn to look at him.*

DOCTOR

No change at all. I 'm sendin' Jane to the drug store.

ELLA (*rises eagerly*)

I 'll just run up and sit with mother.

[*Sadie jumps up and starts for door.*

SADIE

It might be better if I went.

ELLA

Why might it?

[*They stand glaring at each other before either attempts to pass the Doctor, whose ample form almost blocks the doorway.*

SADIE

I 've been a wife and a mother.

DOCTOR

Hannah 's with her, you know. I told you I did n't want anybody up there but Jane and Hannah.

ELLA

But we 're her own daughters.

DOCTOR

You don't have to tell me, I brought both of you into the world. The right nursing might pull her through, even now; nothing else can, and I've got the two women I want. (*He crosses to Henry at stove*) Why don't you put a little wood on the fire?

HENRY

Why — I thought 'twas warm enough.

ELLA

Because you was standin' in front of it gettin' all the heat.

[*Henry fills the stove from wood basket.*

Jane Crosby enters on stairs and crosses into the room. Jane is twenty-four, a plainly dressed girl of quiet manner. She has been "driven into herself" as one of our characters would describe it, by her lack of sympathy and affection and as a natural result she is not especially articulate; she speaks, as a rule, in short sentences, and has cultivated an outward coldness that in the course of time has become almost aggressive.

JANE

I'll go now, Doctor; you'd better go back to her. Hannah's frightened.

DOCTOR

Get it as quick as you can, Jane; I don't know as it's any use, but we've got to keep on tryin'.

JANE

Yes.

[*She exits; Doctor warms his hands.*

DOCTOR

Jane's been up with her three nights. I don't know when I've seen a more dependable girl.

ELLA

She ought to be.

HENRY

If there 's any gratitude in the world.

DOCTOR

Oh, I guess there is; maybe there 'd be more if there
was more reason for it.   It 's awful cold up there,
but I guess I 'll be gettin' back.
[*He crosses toward door.*

HENRY

Doctor!
[*He looks at his watch.*

DOCTOR (*stops in doorway*)

Well?

HENRY

It 's quite a bit past four, I don't suppose — I don't
suppose you can tell ——

DOCTOR

No, I can't tell.
[*He turns and exits up the stairs.*

ELLA

There 's no fool like an old fool.

SADIE

Did you hear him?   " Did n't know when he 'd seen a
more dependable girl than her!"

EMMA

Makes a lot of difference who 's goin' to depend on
her.   I ain't, for one.

NETTIE

If I set out to tell how she 's treated me lots of times,
when I 've come over here to see grandma, nobody
would believe a word of it.

SADIE

Mother took her in out of charity.

ELLA

And kept her out of spite.

HENRY

I don't know as you ought to say that, Ella.

ELLA

It's my place she took, in my own mother's house.
I'd been here now, but for her. I ain't goin' to
forget that. No! Me, all these years payin' board
and slavin' my life out, makin' hats, like a nigger.

NETTIE (*smartly*)

Oh! So *that's* what they're like. I've often won-
dered!

ELLA (*rises*)

You'll keep that common little thing of your wife's
from insultin' me, Henry Jordan, or I won't stay
here another minute.

EMMA (*angry*)

Common!

NETTIE

Mother!

HENRY (*sternly*)

Hush up! All of yer!

SADIE

It's Jane we ought to be talkin' about.

EMMA

Just as soon as you're the head of the family, Henry,
you've got to tell her she ain't wanted here!

HENRY

Well — I don't know as I'd want to do anything that
was n't right. She's been here quite a spell.

SADIE

Eight years!

ELLA

And just a step-cousin, once removed.

HENRY

I guess mother's made her earn her keep. I don't
know as ever there was much love lost between 'em.

EMMA

As soon as your mother's dead, you'll send her
packing.

HENRY

We'll see. I don't like countin' on mother's going;
that way.

SADIE (*hopefully*)

Grandmother lived to eighty-four.

HENRY

All our folks was long lived; nothin' lasts like it
used to, — Poor mother!

ELLA

Of course she'll divide equal, between us three?

HENRY (*doubtfully*)

Well, I don't know!

SADIE

Orin is her only grandchild; she won't forget that.

HENRY

Nettie, there, is just the same as my own. I adopted
her legal, when I married Emma.

EMMA

Of course you did. Your mother's too — just a
woman to make distinctions!

NETTIE

Yes, and the funny part of it is grandma may leave
me a whole lot, for all any of *you* know

ELLA

Nonsense! She 'll divide equally between us three; won't she, Henry?

HENRY (*sadly*)

She 'll do as she pleases, I guess we all know that.

ELLA

She 's a religious woman, she 's *got* to be fair!

HENRY

Well, I guess it would be fair enough if she was to remember the trouble I 've had with my business. I don't know what she 's worth, she's as tight-mouthed as a bear trap, but I could use more'n a third of quite a little sum.

ELLA

Well, you won't get it. Not if I go to law.

EMMA

It 's disgusting. Talking about money at a time like this.

HENRY

I like to see folks reasonable. I don't know what you 'd want of a third of all mother 's got, Ella.

SADIE (*to Ella*)

You, all alone in the world!

ELLA

Maybe I won't be, when I get that money.

SADIE

You don't mean you 'd get married?

EMMA

At your age!

ELLA

I mean I never had anything in all my life; now I 'm going to. I 'm the youngest of all of you, except Ben, and he never was a real Jordan. I 've never had a

chance; I 've been stuck here till I 'm most forty,
worse than if I was dead, fifty times worse!   Now
I 'm going to buy things — everything I want — I
don't care what — I 'll buy it, even if it 's a man!
Anything I want!

NETTIE

A *man!*

[*Nettie looks at Ella in cruel amazement and all but
Orin burst into a laugh — Ella turns up and hides
her face against the window as Orin pulls at his
mother's skirt.*

ORIN

Mum! Mum! I thought you told me not to laugh,
not once, while we was here!

HENRY

You 're right, nephew, and we 're wrong, all of us.
I 'm sorry, Ella, we 're all sorry.

ELLA (*wipes her eyes*)

Laugh if you want to — maybe it won't be so long
before I do some of it myself.

HENRY (*thoughtfully*)

Equally between us three?   Well, poor mother knows
best of course.

[*He sighs.*

SADIE

She would n't leave *him* any, would she, — Ben?

ELLA (*shocked*)

Ben!

HENRY (*in cold anger*)

She 's a woman of her word; no!

SADIE

If he was here he 'd get around her; he always did!

HENRY

Not again!

SADIE

If she ever spoiled anybody it was him, and she 's had to pay for it. Sometimes it looks like it was a sort of a judgment.

HENRY

There has n't been a Jordan, before Ben, who 's disgraced the name·in more 'n a hundred years; he stands indicted before the Grand Jury for some of his drunken devilment. If he had n't run away, like the criminal he is, he 'd be in the State's Prison now, down to Thomaston. Don't talk *Ben* to me, after the way he broke mother's heart, and hurt my credit!

NETTIE

I don't remember him very well. Mother thought it better I should n't come around last time he was here; but he looked real nice in his uniform.

SADIE

It was his bein' born so long after us that made him seem like an outsider; father and mother had n't had any children for years and years! Of course I never want to sit in judgment on my own parents, but I never approved of it; it never seemed quite — what I call proper.

NETTIE (*to Emma*)

Mother, don't you think I 'd better leave the room?

SADIE (*angrily*)

Not if half the stories I 've heard about you are true, I don't.

HENRY

Come, come, no rows! Is this a time or place for spite? We 've always been a united family, we 've always got to be, — leavin' Ben out, of course. You can't make a silk purse out of a sow's ear.

ORIN

Mum! Say Mum! (*He pulls at Sadie's dress*) Why should anybody want to make a silk purse out of a sow's ear?

ELLA

Can't you stop that boy askin' such fool questions?

SADIE

Well, as far as that goes, why should they? It never sounded reasonable to me.

HENRY (*sternly*)

Decent folks don't reason about religion; they just accept it.

ORIN

You could make a skin purse out of a sow's ear, but I 'll be darned if you could make a silk purse out of one. I 'll bet God could n't.

HENRY

Are you going to let him talk about God like that, like he was a real person?

ELLA

I don't know as a body could expect any better; his father was a Baptist!

SADIE (*angrily*)

His father was a good man, and if he talked about God different from what you do, it was because he knew more about him. And as for my being here at all — (*she rises with her arms about Orin*) — I would n't do it, not for anything less than my own mother's deathbed.

HENRY

This family don't ever agree on nothin' but just to differ.

EMMA

As far as I see, the only time you ever get together is when one of you is dead.

ELLA

Maybe that's the reason I got such a feelin' against funerals.

[*The outside door opens and Jane enters, a druggist's bottle in her hand; she is followed by John Bradford, a man of about thirty-five. He is better dressed than any of the others and is a man of a more cosmopolitan type, — a New Englander, but a university man, the local judge and the leading lawyer of the town.*

JANE

I met Judge Bradford on the way.

JUDGE (*John Bradford*)

Court set late. I could n't get here before. Jane tells me that she's very low.

HENRY

Yes.

JUDGE

I can't realize it; she has always been so strong, so dominant.

ELLA

In the midst of life we are in death.

ORIN

Say, Mum, that's in the Bible too!

SADIE

Hush!

ORIN
  Well, ain't it?

SADIE
  Will you hush?

HENRY
  It's our duty to hope so long as we can.

JUDGE
  Yes, of course.

JANE
  I'll take this right up.
  [*She exits up the stairs.*

JUDGE (*removes his coat*)
  I'll wait.

SADIE
  She can't see you; she ain't really what a body could
  call in her right mind.

JUDGE
  So Jane said.
  [*He crosses to stove and warms his hands.*

ELLA (*sighs*)
  It's a sad time for us, Judge!

JUDGE
  She was always such a wonderful woman.

HENRY
  An awful time for us.   Did you come up Main Street,
  Judge?

JUDGE
  Yes.

HENRY
  Did you happen to notice if my store was open?

JUDGE
  No.

HENRY

Not that it matters ——

SADIE

Nothing matters now.

HENRY

No — Mother was n't ever the kind to neglect things ; if the worst does come she 'll find herself prepared. Won't she?   Won't she, Judge?

JUDGE

Her affairs are, as usual, in perfect order.

HENRY

In every way?

JUDGE (*looks at him coldly*)

Her will is drawn and is on deposit in my office, if that is what you mean.

HENRY

Well — that *is* what I mean — I 'm no hypocrite.

EMMA

He 's the oldest of the family.   He 's got a right to ask, has n't he?

JUDGE

Yes.

HENRY (*honestly*)

If I could make her well by givin' up everything I 've got in the world, or ever expect to git, I 'd do it!

SADIE

All of us would.

HENRY

If it 's in my mind at all, as I stand here, that she 's a rich woman, it 's because my mind 's so worried, the way business has been, that I 'm drove most frantic ; it 's because, well — because I 'm human ; because I can't help it.

ELLA (*bitterly*)

You 're a man! What do you think it 's been for me!

SADIE (*with arm about Orin*)

His father did n't leave much, you all know that, and it 's been scrimp and save till I 'm all worn to skin and bone.

ELLA

Just to the three of us, that would be fair.

HENRY

Judge! My brother's name ain't in her will, is it? Tell me that? Ben's name ain't there!

JUDGE

I 'd rather not talk about it, Henry.

ELLA

She 'd cut him off, she said, the last time he disgraced us, and she 's a woman of her word.

SADIE (*eagerly, to Judge*)

And the very next day she sent for you because I was here when she telephoned; and you came to her that very afternoon because I saw you from my front window cross right up to this door.

JUDGE

Possibly. I frequently drop in to discuss business matters with your mother for a moment on my way home.

SADIE

It was five minutes to four when you went in that day, and six minutes to five when you came out, by the clock on my mantel.

JUDGE

Your brother has been gone for almost two years; Your memory is very clear.

ELLA

So 's her window.

NETTIE

I know folks in this town that are scared to go past it.

SADIE (*to her*)

I know others that ought to be.

HENRY (*discouraged*)

Every time you folks meet there 's trouble.

[*Jane enters down the stairs and into the room.*

JUDGE (*looks at her*)

Well, Jane?

JANE

No change.   It 's — it 's pitiful, to see her like that.

[*Sadie sobs and covers her face.*

HENRY

It 's best we should try to bear this without any fuss, she 'd 'a' wanted it that way.

SADIE

She did n't even want me to cry when poor Will died, but I did; and somehow I don't know but it made things easier.

HENRY

When father died she did n't shed a tear; she 's been a strong woman, always.

[*The early fall twilight has come on and the stage is rather dim, the hall at R. is in deep shadow, at the end of Henry's speech the outside door supposedly out at R. is open, then shut rather violently.*

ELLA (*startled*)

Someone 's come in.

SADIE

Nobody 's got any right ——

[*She rises as some one is heard coming along the hall.*

HENRY (*sternly*)

Who's that out there?   Who is it?

ORIN

Mum!   Who is it!

[*He clings to his mother afraid, as all turn to the door, and Ben Jordan steps into the room and faces them with a smile of reckless contempt. Ben is the black sheep of the Jordan family, years younger than any of the others, a wild, selfish, arrogant fellow, handsome but sulky and defiant. His clothes are cheap and dirty and he is rather pale and looks dissipated. He doesn't speak but stands openly sneering at their look of astonishment.*

JANE (*quietly*)

I'm glad you've come, Ben.

BEN (*contemptuously*)

You are?

JANE

Yes, your mother's awful sick.

BEN

She's alive?

JANE

Yes.

BEN

Well — (*He looks contemptuously about*)
Nobody missin'.   The Jordans are gathered again, handkerchiefs and all.

HENRY

You'll be arrested soon as folks know you've come.

BEN (*scornfully*)

And I suppose you wouldn't bail me out, would you, Henry?

HENRY (*simply*)

　No, I would n't.

BEN

　God! You 're still the same, all of you. You stink
　of the Ark, the whole tribe. It takes more than a
　few Edisons to change the Jordans!

ELLA

　How 'd you get here? How 'd you know about
　mother?

BEN (*nods at Jane*)

　She sent me word, to Bangor.

SADIE (*to Jane*)

　How 'd you get to know where he was?

JANE (*quietly*)

　I knew.

HENRY

　How 'd you come; you don't look like you had much
　money?

BEN

　She sent it. (*He nods toward Jane*) God knows, it
　was n't much.

ELLA (*to Jane*)

　Did mother tell you to ——?

BEN

　Of course she did!

JANE (*quietly*)

　No, she did n't.

HENRY

　You sent your own money?

JANE

　Yes, as he said it was n't much, but I did n't have
　much.

BEN (*astonished*)

Why did you do it?

JANE

I knew she was going to die; twice I asked her if she wanted to see you, and she said no ——

HENRY

And yet you sent for him?

JANE

Yes.

HENRY

Why?

JANE

He was the one she really wanted. I thought she'd die happier seeing him.

ELLA

You took a lot on yourself, did n't you?

JANE

Yes, she's been a lonely old woman. I hated to think of her there, in the churchyard, hungry for him.

BEN

I'll go to her.

JANE

It's too late; she would n't know you.

BEN

I'll go.

JANE

The doctor will call us when he thinks we ought to come.

BEN (*fiercely*)

I'm going now.

HENRY (*steps forward*)

No, you ain't.

BEN

Do you think I came here, standin' a chance of bein' sent to jail, to let *you* tell me what to do?

HENRY

If she 's dyin' up there, it 's more 'n half from what you 've made her suffer; you 'll wait here till we go to her together.

EMMA

Henry 's right.

SADIE

Of course he is.

ELLA

Nobody but Ben would have the impudence to show his face here, after what he 's done.

BEN

I 'm going just the same!

HENRY

No, you ain't.

[*Their voices become loud.*

EMMA

Henry! Don't let him go!

SADIE

Stop him.

ELLA (*grows shrill*)

He 's a disgrace to us. He always was.

HENRY

You 'll stay right where you are.

[*He puts his hand heavily on Ben's shoulder—Ben throws him off fiercely.*

BEN

Damn you! Keep your hands off me!

[*Henry staggers back and strikes against a table that falls to the floor with a crash. Nettie screams.*

JANE

Stop it — stop! You must!

JUDGE

Are you crazy? Have you no sense of decency?

[*Doctor Curtis comes quickly downstairs.*

DOCTOR

What 's this noise? I forbid it. Your mother has heard you.

HENRY (*ashamed*)

I 'm sorry.

BEN (*sulkily*)

I did n't mean to make a row.

HENRY

It 's him. (*He looks bitterly at Ben*) He brings out all the worst in us. He brought trouble into the world with him when he came, and ever since.

[*Hannah, a middle-aged servant, comes hastily half-way downstairs and calls out sharply.*

HANNAH

Doctor! Come, Doctor!

[*She exits up the stairs, as the Doctor crosses through the hall and follows her.*

ORIN (*afraid*)

Is she dead, Mum? Does Hannah mean she 's dead!

[*Sadie hides her head on his shoulder and weeps.*

JANE

I 'll go to her.

[*She exits.*

ELLA (*violently*)

She 'll go. There ain't scarcely a drop of Jordan blood in her veins, and *she 's* the one that goes to mother.

EMMA (*coldly*)

Light the lamp, Nettie; it's gettin' dark.

NETTIE

Yes, mother.

[*She starts to light lamp.*

HENRY

I'm ashamed of my part of it, makin' a row, with her on her deathbed.

BEN

You had it right, I guess. I've made trouble ever since I came into the world.

NETTIE

There!

[*She lights lamp; footlights go up.*

JUDGE (*sternly*)

You should n't have come here; you know that, Ben.

BEN

I've always known that, any place I've been, exceptin' only those two years in the Army. That's the only time I ever was in right.

JUDGE (*sternly*)

I would find it easier to pity you if you had any one to blame besides yourself.

BEN

Pity? Do you think I want your pity?

[*There is a pause.*

Jane is seen on stairs, they all turn to her nervously as she comes down and crosses into room. She stops at the door looking at them.

HENRY (*slowly*)

Mother — mother's — gone!

JANE

Yes.

[*There is a moment's silence broken by the low sobs of the women who for a moment forget their selfishness in the presence of death.*

HENRY

The Jordans won't ever be the same; she was the last of the old stock, mother was — No, the Jordans won't ever be the same.

[*Doctor Curtis comes downstairs and into the room.*

DOCTOR

It's no use tryin' to tell you what I feel. I've known her since I was a boy. I did the best I could.

HENRY

The best anybody could, Doctor, we know that.

DOCTOR

I've got a call I'd better make — (*He looks at watch*) — should have been there hours ago, but I had n't the heart to leave her. Who's in charge here?

HENRY

I am, of course.

DOCTOR

I've made arrangements with Hannah; she'll tell you.

I'll say good night now.

HENRY

Good night, Doctor.

JANE

And thank you.

DOCTOR

We did our best, Jane.

[*He exits.*

SADIE

He's gettin' old. When Orin had the stomach trouble a month ago, I sent for Doctor Morris. I felt sort of guilty doin' it, but I thought it was my duty.

JUDGE

You will let me help you, Jane?

JANE

Hannah and I can attend to everything. Henry! (*She turns to him*) You might come over for a minute this evening and we can talk things over. I'll make the bed up in your old room, Ben, if you want to stay.

EMMA (*rises and looks at Jane coldly*)

Now, Henry Jordan, if she's all through givin' orders, maybe you'll begin.

ELLA

Well, I should say so. Let's have an understandin'.

SADIE

You tell her the truth, Henry, or else one of us will do it for you.

HENRY (*hesitates*)

Maybe it might be best if I should wait until after the funeral.

ELLA

You tell her now, or I will.

JANE

Tell me what?

HENRY

We was thinkin' now that mother's dead, that there wasn't much use in your stayin' on here.

JANE

Yes?

[*She looks at him intently*

HENRY

We don't aim to be hard, and we don't want it said we was mean about it; you can stay on here, if you want to, until after the funeral, maybe a little longer, and I don't know but what between us, we'd be willing to help you till you found a place somewheres.

JANE

You can't help me, any of you. Of course now she's dead, I'll go. I'll be glad to go.

ELLA

Glad!

JANE (*turns on them*)

I hate you, the whole raft of you. I'll be glad to get away from you. She was the only one of you worth loving, and she did n't want it.

EMMA

If that's how you feel, I say the sooner you went the better.

HENRY

Not till after the funeral. I don't want it said we was hard to her.

JUDGE (*quietly*)

Jane is n't going at all, Henry.

HENRY

What's that?

ELLA

Of course she's going.

JUDGE

No, she belongs here in this house.

HENRY

Not after I say she don't.

JUDGE

Even then, because it 's hers.

SADIE

Hers?

JUDGE

From the moment of your mother's death, everything here belonged to Jane.

HENRY

Not everything.

JUDGE

Yes, everything — your mother's whole estate.

BEN

Ha! Ha! Ha!

[*He sits at right laughing bitterly.*

JANE

That can't be, Judge, you must be wrong. It 's a mistake.

JUDGE

No.

HENRY

My mother did this?

JUDGE

Yes.

HENRY

Why? You 've got to tell me why!

JUDGE

That is n't a part of my duties.

HENRY

She could n't have done a thing like that without sayin' why. She said something, did n't she?

JUDGE

I don't know that I care to repeat it.

HENRY (*fiercely*)

You must repeat it!

JUDGE

Very well. The day that will was drawn she said to me, " The Jordans are all waiting for me to die, like carrion crows around a sick cow in a pasture, watchin' till the last twitch of life is out of me before they pounce. I'm going to fool them," she said, " I'm going to surprise them; they are all fools but Jane — Jane's no fool."

BEN (*bitterly*)

No — Ha! Ha! Ha! Jane 's no fool!

JUDGE

And she went on — (*He turns to Jane*) You 'll forgive me Jane; she said, " Jane is stubborn, and set, and wilful, but she 's no fool. She 'll do better by the Jordan money than any of them."

ELLA

We 'll go to law, that 's what we 'll do!

SADIE

That 's it, we 'll go to law.

HENRY (*to Judge*)

We can break that will; you know we can!

JUDGE

It 's possible.

HENRY

Possible! You *know*, don't yer! You 're supposed to be a good lawyer.

JUDGE

Of course if I *am* a good lawyer you can't break that will, because you see I drew it.

ELLA

And we get nothing, not a dollar, after waitin' all these years?

JUDGE

There are small bequests left to each of you.

SADIE

How much?

JUDGE

One hundred dollars each.

ELLA (*shrilly*)

One hundred dollars.

JUDGE

I said that they were small.

BEN

You said a mouthful!

ELLA

Ha! Ha! Ha! Ha! Ha!
[*She laughs wildly.*

HENRY (*sternly*)

Stop your noise, Ella.

ELLA

I —— Ha! Ha! Ha! —— I told you I was going to have my laugh, did n't I? Ha! Ha! Ha!

ORIN (*pulls Sadie's dress*)

Mum! What 's she laughin' for?

SADIE

You hush!

EMMA (*faces them all in evil triumph*)

If anybody asked me, I 'd say it was a judgment on all of yer. You Jordans was always stuck up, always thought you was better 'n anybody else. I guess I ought to know, I married into yer! — You a

rich family? — You the salt of the Earth — You
Jordans! You paupers — Ha! Ha! Ha!

ORIN (*pulls Sadie's skirt*)

Ain't she still dead, Mum! Ain't grandma still dead?

SADIE (*angrily*)

Of course she is.

ORIN

But I thought we was all goin' to cry!

SADIE

Cry then, you awful little brat.

[*She slaps his face and he roars loudly; she takes
him by the arm and yanks him out of the room,
followed by Henry, Emma, Nettie and Ella —
through his roars, they all speak together as they go.*

EMMA (*to Henry*)

One hundred dollars! After all your blowin'.

HENRY

It's you, and that child of your 'n; you turned her
against me.

NETTIE

Well, I just won't spend my hundred dollars for
mournin'. I'll wear my old black dress!

ELLA

And me makin' hats all the rest of my life — just
makin' hats!

[*The front door is heard to shut behind them. Jane,
Ben and Judge are alone. Judge stands by stove.
Jane is up by window, looking out at the deepening
twilight. Ben sits at right.*

BEN

Ha! Ha! Ha! "Crow buzzards" mother called us
— the last of the Jordans — crow buzzards — and
that's what we are.

JUDGE

You can't stay here, Ben; you know that as well as
I do. I signed the warrant for your arrest myself.
It's been over a vear since the Grand Jury indicted
you for arson.

BEN

You mean you'll give me up?

JANE

You won't do that, Judge; you're here as her friend.

JUDGE

No, but if it's known he's here, I could n't save him,
and it's bound to be known.

JANE (*to Ben*)

Were you careful coming?

BEN

Yes.

JUDGE

It's bound to be known.

BEN

He means they'll tell on me. (*He nods his head
toward door*) My brother, or my sisters.

JUDGE

No, I don't think they'd do that.

BEN

Let 'em! What do I care. I'm sick of hiding out,
half starved! Let 'em do what they please. All I
know is one thing, — when they put her into her
grave her sons and daughters are goin' to be standin'
there, like the Jordans always do.

JANE (*quietly*)

Hannah will have your room ready by now. There
are some clean shirts and things that was your
father's; I'll bring them to you.

BEN (*uneasily*)

Can I go up there, just a minute?

JANE

To your mother?

BEN

Yes.

JANE

If you want to.

BEN

I do.

JANE

Yes, you can go.

[*Ben turns and exits up the stairs. Jane crosses
and sits by stove, sinking wearily into the chair.*

JUDGE

And she left him nothing, just that hundred dollars,
and only that because I told her it was the safest
way to do it. I thought he was her one weakness,
but it seems she did n't have any.

JANE

No.

JUDGE

She was a grim old woman, Jane.

JANE

I think I could have loved her, but she did n't want it.

JUDGE

And yet she left you everything.

JANE

I don't understand.

JUDGE

She left a sealed letter for you. It 's in my strong
box; you may learn from it that she cared more
about you than you think.

JANE

No.

JUDGE

There was more kindness in her heart than most
people gave her credit for.

JANE

For her own, for Uncle Ned, who never did for her,
for Ned, for the Jordan name. I don't understand,
and I don't think I care so very much; it's been a
hard week, Judge.

[*She rests her head against the back of the chair.*

JUDGE

I know, and you're all worn out.

JANE

Yes.

JUDGE

It's a lot of money, Jane.

JANE

I suppose so.

JUDGE

And so you're a rich woman. I am curious to know
how you feel?

JANE

Just tired.

[*She shuts her eyes. For a moment he looks at her
with a smile, then turns and quietly fills the stove
with wood as Ben comes slowly downstairs and into
the room.*

BEN

If there was only something I could do for her.

JUDGE

Jane's asleep, Ben.

BEN

Did she look like that, unhappy, all the time?

JUDGE

Yes.

BEN

Crow buzzards! God damn the Jordans!

[*Front door bell rings sharply, Ben is startled.*

JUDGE

Steady there! It's just one of the neighbors, I guess. (*Bell rings again as Hannah crosses downstairs and to hall*)   Hannah knows enough not to let any one in.

BEN (*slowly*)

When I got back, time before this, from France, I tried to go straight, but it was n't any good, I just don't belong ——

[*Hannah enters frightened.*

HANNAH

It's Jim Jay!

BEN (*to Judge*)

And you did n't think my own blood would sell me?

[*Jim Jay, a large, kindly man of middle age, enters.*

JIM

I'm sorry, Ben, I've come for you!

[*Jane wakes, startled, and springs up.*

JANE

What is it?

JIM

I got to take him, Jane.

BEN (*turns fiercely*)

Have you!

JIM (*quietly*)

I'm armed, Ben — better not be foolish!

JANE

He'll go with you, Mr. Jay. He won't resist.

JIM (*quietly*)

He mustn't. You got a bad name, Ben, and I ain't a-goin' to take any chances.

BEN

I thought I'd get to go to her funeral, anyway, before they got me.

JIM

Well, you could, maybe, if you was to fix a bail bond. You'd take bail for him, wouldn't you, Judge?

JUDGE

It's a felony; I'd have to have good security.

JANE

I'm a rich woman, you said just now. Could I give bail for him?

JUDGE

Yes.

BEN (*to her*)

So the money ain't enough. You want all us Jordans fawnin' on you for favors. Well, all of 'em but me will; by mornin' the buzzards will be flocking round you thick! You're going to hear a lot about how much folks love you, but you ain't goin' to hear it from me.

JANE (*turns to him quietly*)

Why did you come here, Ben, when I wrote you she was dying?

BEN

Why did I come?

JANE

Was it because you loved her, because you wanted to

ask her to forgive you, before she died — or was it because you wanted to get something for yourself?

BEN (*hesitates*)

How does a feller know why he does what he does?

JANE

I 'm just curious. You 've got so much contempt for the rest, I was just wondering? You were wild, Ben, and hard, but you were honest — what brought you here?

BEN (*sulkily*)

The money.

JANE

I thought so. Then when you saw her you were sorry, but even then the money was in your mind — well — it 's mine now. And you 've got to take your choice, — you can do what I tell you, or you 'll go with Mr. Jay.

BEN

Is that so? Well I guess there ain't much doubt about what I 'll do. Come on, Jim?

JIM

All right. (*He takes a pair of handcuffs from his pocket*) You 'll have to slip these on, Ben.

BEN (*steps back*)

No — wait — (*He turns desperately to Jane*) What is it you want?

JANE

I want you to do as I say.

BEN (*after a look at Jim and the handcuffs*)

I 'll do it.

JANE

I thought so. (*She turns to Judge*) Can you fix the bond up here?

JUDGE

Yes. (*He sits at table and takes pen, ink and paper from a drawer*) I can hold court right here long enough for that.

JIM

This is my prisoner, Judge, and here's the warrant. [*He puts warrant on table.*

JANE

First he's got to swear, before you, to my conditions.

BEN

What conditions?

JANE

When will his trial be, Judge?

JUDGE

Not before the spring term, I should think — say early April.

JANE

You'll stay here till then, Ben; you won't leave town! You'll work the farm, — there's plenty to be done.

BEN (*sulkily*)

I don't know how to work a farm.

JANE

I do. You'll just do what I tell you.

BEN

Be your slave? That's what you mean, ain't it?

JANE

I've been about that here for eight years.

BEN

And now it's your turn to get square on a Jordan!

JANE

You'll work for once, and work every day. The first day you don't I'll surrender you to the judge, and he'll jail you. The rest of the Jordans will live as I tell them to live, or for the first time in any of their lives, they 'll live on what they earn.   Don't forget, Ben, that right now I 'm the head of the family.

JUDGE (*to Ben*)

You heard the conditions?   Shall I make out the bond?

BEN (*reluctantly*)

Yes.

[*He sits moodily at right, looking down at the floor. Jane looks at him for a moment, then turns up to window.*

JANE

It 's snowing!

JIM

Thought I smelled it.   (*He buttons his coat*)   Well, nothin' to keep me, is there, Judge?

JUDGE

No.   (*He starts to write out the bond with a rusty pen*)   This pen is rusty!

JIM

I was sorry to hear about the old lady.   It 's too bad, but that 's the way of things.

JUDGE (*writes*)

Yes.

JIM

Well — It 's early for snow, not but what it 's a good thing for the winter wheat.

[*He exits.*

CURTAIN

ACT TWO

Scene: Sitting room of the Jordan homestead some two months later.

This room also shows some traces of a family's daily life, and to that extent is less desolate than the "parlor" of the first act, although the stern faith of the Puritan makes no concession to the thing we have learned to call "good taste." The old-fashioned simplicity seen in such a room as this has resulted from poverty, both of mind and of purse, and has nothing akin to the simplicity of the artist; as a matter of fact, your true descendant of the settlers of 1605 would be the first to resent such an implication; to them the arts are directly connected with heathen practices, and any incense burned before the altars of the Graces still smells to them of brimstone.

At back center folding doors, now partly open, lead to dining room. In this room may be seen the dining table, back of the table a window looking out on to the farm yard, now deep in midwinter snow. At right is an open fireplace with a log fire. Below fireplace a door to hall. Up left door to small vestibule in which is the outside door. Down left a window overlooking a snowbound countryside. The clock above the fireplace is set for quarter past four. Several straight-backed chairs and a woodbox by fireplaces. A sewing table and lamp at center. A sewing machine near win-

*dow at left. A wall cupboard on the wall right of the
doors to the dining room. An old sofa down left, two
chairs at right. When the door at left, in vestibule, is
opened, one may see a path up to the door, between two
walls of snow.*

*Discovered: Ella sits right at sewing machine, hem-
ming some rough towels. Orin and Nettie are by fireplace. Sadie sits right of center. Sadie and Orin are
dressed for outdoors. Nettie's coat, hat and overshoes
are on a hat-rack by door at left. Orin, as the curtain
goes up, is putting a log on the fire.*

SADIE (*acidly to Ella*)

Why should n't he put wood on the fire if he
wants to?

ELLA (*at sewing machine*)

Because it ain't your wood.

SADIE

No, it 's *hers!* Everything is hers!

ELLA

And maybe she just don't know it.

NETTIE (*at fireplace*)

Ah! (*She bends closer to the fire as the log blazes
up*) I do love a good fire! Oh it 's nice to be warm!

SADIE

There 's somethin' sensual about it.

NETTIE

Mother told me that the next time you started talkin'
indecent I was to leave the room.

SADIE

Tell your mother I don't wonder she 's sort of worried about you. I 'd be if you was *my* daughter.

ELLA

I don't see why you can't let Nettie alone!

NETTIE

She's always picking on me, Aunt Ella! To hear her talk anybody would think I was terrible.

SADIE

I know more about what's going on than some folks think I do.

NETTIE

Then you know a lot. I heard Horace Bevins say a week ago that he did n't know as it was any use tryin' to have a Masonic Lodge in the same town as you.

SADIE

They never was a Bevins yet did n't have his tongue hung from the middle; the day his mother was married she answered both the responses.

ORIN

Mum! Mum! Shall I take my coat off; are we going to stay, Mum?

SADIE

No, we ain't going to stay. I just want to see Cousin Jane for a minute.

ELLA

She's in the kitchen with Hannah.

SADIE

Watchin' her, I bet! I wonder Hannah puts up with it.

ELLA

If you was to live with Jane for a spell, I guess you 'd find you had a plenty to put up with.

SADIE

It's enough to make the Jordans turn in their graves, all of 'em at once.

ELLA

I guess all she 'd say would be, " Let 'em if it seemed to make 'em any more comfortable."

[*Jane enters. She has apron on and some towels over her arm.*

JANE

Are those towels finished?

ELLA

Some is! Maybe I 'd done all of 'em if I 'd been a centipede.

JANE

Oh! I did n't see you, Sadie.

SADIE

Oh! Ha, ha! Well, I ain't surprised.

JANE (*with Ella, selecting finished towels*) Well, Orin, does the tooth still hurt you?

ORIN

Naw, it don't hurt me none now. I got it in a bottle.

[*He takes small bottle from pocket.*

NETTIE

Oh you nasty thing. You get away!

SADIE (*angrily*)

What did I tell you about showin' that tooth to folks!

JANE

Never mind, Orin, just run out to the barn and tell your Uncle Ben we 've got to have a path cleared under the clothes-lines.

ORIN

All right.

[*He crosses toward door.*

JANE

Hannah's going to wash to-morrow, tell him. I'll expect a good wide path.

ORIN

I'll tell him.

[*He exits.*

SADIE

I must say you keep Ben right at it, don't you?

JANE

Yes. (*She takes the last finished towel and speaks to Ella*) I'll come back for more.

SADIE (*as Jane crosses*)

First I thought he'd go to jail before he'd work, but he did n't, did he?

JANE

No.

[*She exits right.*

SADIE

Yes. No! Yes. No! Folks that ain't got no more gift of gab ain't got much gift of intellect. I s'pose Hannah's out there.

ELLA

Yes, she keeps all of us just everlastingly at it.

SADIE

When Jane comes back, I wish you and Nettie would leave me alone with her, just for a minute.

ELLA (*as she works over sewing machine*)

It won't do you much good; she won't lend any more money.

SADIE

Mother always helped me. I've got a right to expect it.

ELLA (*as she bites off a thread*)
Expectin' ain't gettin'.

SADIE
I don't know what I 'll do.

ELLA
You had money out of her; so has Henry.

SADIE (*shocked, to Nettie*)
You don't mean to say your father 's been borrowin'
from her.
[*This to Nettie.*

NETTIE
He 's always borrowin'. Did n't he borrow the hundred dollars grandma left me? I 'm not going to
stand it much longer.

ELLA
Henry 's havin' trouble with his business.

SADIE
We 're fools to put up with it. Everybody says so.
We ought to contest the will.

ELLA
Everybody says so but the lawyers; they won't none
of 'em touch the case without they get money in
advance.

SADIE
How much money? Did n't your father find out,
Nettie?

NETTIE
The least was five hundred dollars.

ELLA
Can you see us raisin' that?

SADIE
If we was short, we might borrow it from Jane.

ELLA

We 'd have to be smarter 'n I see any signs of; she 's through lendin'.

SADIE

How do you know?

ELLA

I tried it myself.

SADIE

What do you want money for. Ain't she takin' you in to live with her?

ELLA

I don't call myself beholden for that. She had to have some one, with Ben here, and her unmarried, and next to no relation to him.

NETTIE

Everybody 's callin' you the chaperon! (*She laughs*) Not but what they ought to be one with *him* around; he 's awful good lookin'.

SADIE

You keep away from him. He 's no blood kin of yours, and he 's a bad man, if he is a Jordan. Always makes up to everything he sees in petticoats, and always did.

NETTIE

Thanks for the compliment, but I 'm not looking for any jailbirds.

ELLA

It will be awful, Ben in State's Prison, — and I guess he 'll have to go, soon as he stands his trial.

SADIE

He got drunk and had a fight with the two Kimbal boys, and they licked him, and that night he burned down their barn; everybody knows it.

ELLA

He 's bad, all through, Ben is.

NETTIE

He 'll get about five years, father says. I guess that
will take some of the spunk out of him.
[*A sound in the hall at right.*

ELLA

Hush! I think he 's coming.
[*Ben enters at right with a big armful of firewood
and crosses and drops it heavily into woodbox, then
turns and looks at them in silence.*

SADIE

Seems kind of funny, your luggin' in the wood.

BEN (*bitterly*)

Does it?

SADIE

Did you see Orin out there?

BEN

Yes, he went along home.

SADIE

How do you like workin'?

BEN

How do you think I like it? Workin' a big farm in
winter, tendin' the stock and milking ten cows. How
do I like it?
[*As he stands by fire Nettie looks up at him.*

NETTIE

I think it 's just a shame!

SADIE (*turns to Ella*)

Are you going to make towels all the afternoon?

ELLA

I am 'til they 're done, then I expect she 'll find somethin' else for me to do.

NETTIE (*to Ben*)

Do you know I'm sorry for you, awful sorry.

[*She speaks low. Ella and Sadie are at the other side of room.*

BEN

Then you're the only one.

NETTIE

Maybe I am, but I'm like that.

BEN

Another month of it, then State's Prison, I guess. I don't know as I'll be sorry when the time comes.

NETTIE

Oh, Uncle Ben! No, I'm not goin' to call you *that*. After all, you're not really any relation, are you? I mean to me?

BEN

No.

NETTIE (*softly*)

I'm just going to call you Ben!

BEN

You're a good kid, Nettie.

NETTIE

Oh, it isn't that, Ben, but it does just seem too awful.

[*As she looks up at him, the outside door opens and Henry and Emma enter. They see Nettie and Ben together by the fire.*

EMMA (*sternly*)

Nettie!

NETTIE (*sweetly*)

Yes, mother?

EMMA

You come away from him.

BEN (*angrily*)
    What do you mean by that?

EMMA
    You tell him, Henry.

HENRY
    I don't know as it 's any use to ——

EMMA (*sternly*)
    Tell him what I mean.

HENRY (*to Ben*)
    Emma thinks, considerin' everything, that it 's best
    Nettie should n't talk to you.

BEN
    Why don't you keep her at home then?   You don't
    suppose I want to talk to her.

EMMA
    Oh, we ain't wanted here, I guess.   We know that,
    not by you, or by *her;* — and Henry 's the oldest of
    the Jordans.   All this would be his, if there was any
    justice in the world.

NETTIE
    Father would n't have taken that hundred dollars
    grandma left me if there had been any justice in the
    world.   That 's what I came here for, not to talk to
    him.   To tell Cousin Jane what father did, and to tell
    her about Nellie Namlin's Christmas party, and
    that I 've got to have a new dress.   I 've just got
    to !

SADIE
    A new dress, and my rent ain't paid.   She 's got to
    pay it.   My Orin 's got to have a roof over his head.

HENRY

I don't know as you 've got any call to be pestering
Jane all the time.

ELLA

She 's always wantin' something.

SADIE

What about you? Did n't you tell me yourself you
tried to borrow from her?

ELLA

I got a chance to set up in business, so as I can be
independent. I can go in with Mary Stanton, dress-
makin'. I can do it for two hundred dollars, and
she 's got to give it to me.

HENRY

You ought to be ashamed, all three of you, worryin'
Jane all day long. It 's more 'n flesh and blood can
stand!

NETTIE (*to him*)

Did n't you say at breakfast you was coming here
to-day to make Cousin Jane endorse a note for you?
Did n't you?

EMMA (*fiercely*)

You hush!

BEN (*at back by window*)

Ha! Ha! Ha! Crow buzzards.

HENRY

Endorsing a note ain't lending money, is it? It 's a
matter of business. I guess my note 's good.

BEN

Take it to the bank without her name on it and see
how good it is.

EMMA

You don't think we want to ask her favors, but Henry's in bad trouble and she'll just have to help us this time.

BEN

There's one way out of your troubles. One thing you could all do, for a change, instead of making Jane pay all your bills. I wonder you have n't any of you thought of it.

HENRY

What could we do?

BEN

Go to work and earn something for yourselves.

SADIE

Like you do, I suppose.

EMMA

The laughing-stock of all Veazie!

ELLA

Everybody's talkin' about it, anywhere you go.

NETTIE

Jane Crosby's White Slave, that's what they call you. Jane Crosby's White Slave.

BEN (*fiercely*)

They call me that, do they?

ELLA (*to Nettie*)

Why can't you ever hold your tongue?

BEN (*in cold anger*)

I've been a damned fool. I'm through.

[*Hannah enters.*

HANNAH

She wants you.

BEN

Jane?

HANNAH

Yes.

BEN

I won't come.

HANNAH

There 'll be another row.

BEN

Tell her I said I would n't come.
[*He sits.*

HANNAH

She 's awful set, you know, when she wants anything.

BEN

You tell her I won't come.

HANNAH

Well, I don't say I hanker none to tell her, but I 'd
rather be in my shoes than yourn.
[*She exits.*

SADIE

Well, I must say I don't blame you a mite.

EMMA

If the Jordans is a lot of slaves, I guess it 's pretty
near time we knew it.

HENRY (*worried*)

She 'll turn you over to Judge Bradford, Ben; he 'll
lock you up. It ain't goin' to help me none with the
bank, a brother of mine bein' in jail.

BEN

So they 're laughing at me, are they, damn them.

NETTIE (*at door right*)

She 's coming!
[*There is a moment's pause and Jane enters door
right. Hannah follows to door and looks on eagerly.*

JANE

I sent for you, Ben.

BEN

I won't budge.

JANE (*wearily*)

Must we go through all this again?

BEN

I ain't going to move out of this chair to-day. You do what you damned please.

JANE

I am sorry, but you must.

BEN

Send for Jim Jay, have me locked up, do as you please. Oh, I've said it before, but this time I mean it.

JANE

And you won't come?

BEN

No.

JANE

Then I'll do the best I can alone.

[*She crosses up to wall closet and opens it and selects a large bottle, and turns. Ben rises quickly.*

BEN

What do you want of that?

JANE

It's one of the horses. I don't know what's the matter with her. She's down in her stall, just breathing. She won't pay any attention to me.

BEN

Old Nellie?

JANE

Yes.

BEN

What you got? (*He steps to her and takes the bottle from her and looks at it*) That stuff's no good. Here! (*He steps to cabinet and selects another bottle*) If you had n't spent five minutes stalling around, I might have had a better chance.
[*He exits quickly at left.*

HANNAH

I allers said 't was easier to catch flies with honey than•'t was with vinegar.

HENRY

What's Ben know about horses?

JANE

A lot.

HENRY

I did n't know that.

JANE

Neither did Ben, six weeks ago.
[*She exits.*

HENRY

Mother was like that, about animals. I guess Ben sort of takes after her.

EMMA (*shocked*)

Ben! Like your mother!

HANNAH

Of course he is. He's the " spit and image of her."
[*She exits.*

NETTIE

She made him go! It would n't surprise me a mite if she 'd pushed that old horse over herself.
[*Jane enters.*

JANE

He would n't let me in the barn. (*For the first time in the play, she laughs lightly*) Well — (*She looks about at them*) we have quite a family gathering here this afternoon. I am wondering if there is any — special reason for it?

HENRY

I wanted to talk with yer for just a minute, Jane.

SADIE

So do I.

JANE

Anybody else?
[*She looks about.*

ELLA

I do.

NETTIE

So do I.

JANE

I 've a lot to do; suppose I answer you all at once. I 'm sorry, but I won't lend you any money.

HENRY

Of course, I did n't think they 'd call that note of mine; it 's only five hundred, and you could just endorse it.

JANE

No!

SADIE

I was going to ask you ——

JANE

No!

ELLA

I got a chance to be independent, Jane, and ——
No. I have n't any money. I won't have before the
first of the month.

EMMA

No money!

HENRY

I bet you 're worth as much to-day as you was the
day mother died.

JANE

To a penny. I 've lived, and run this house, and half
supported all of you on what I 've made the place
earn. Yesterday I spent the first dollar that I
did n't have to spend. I mean, on myself. But
that 's no business of yours. I *am* worth just as
much as the day I took the property, and I 'm not
going to run behind, so you see, after all, I 'm a real
Jordan.

EMMA

Seems so. I never knew one of 'em yet who did n't
seem to think he could take it with him.

HENRY

Well, Jane, I don't know as it 's any use tryin' to
get you to change your mind?

JANE

I 'm sorry.

EMMA

You can leave that for us to be. I guess it 's about
the only thing we 've got a right to. Get your things
on, Nettie!

NETTIE

I 'm going to stay a while with Aunt Ella; I won't
be late.

HENRY

I don't know what I 'm goin' to do about that note.
I s 'pose I 'll find some way out of it.

JANE

I hope so.

EMMA

Thank yer. Of course we know there 's always the
poorhouse. Come, Henry.
[*She exits at left, leaving the outside door open.*

HENRY

Emma is a little upset. I hope you won't mind her
talk. I guess her part of it ain't any too easy.
[*He exits, shutting the door.*

ELLA (*to Jane*)

Poor Henry! Of course I s 'pose you 're right not
to lend it to him. But I don't know as I could do it,
but I 'm sensitive.

JANE

Perhaps it 's harder to say no than you think.
[*Hannah enters.*

HANNAH

I got everything ready for to-morrow's wash, but the
sheets off your bed, Miss Ella.

ELLA

Good Land! I forgot 'em. Nettie will bring 'em
right down.

NETTIE (*to Jane*)

After that, I 'm going to stay and help Aunt Ella.
I was wondering if you 'd be here all the afternoon.

JANE

Yes.

NETTIE (*charmingly*)

Nothing special, you know. I'd just like to have a little visit with you.

[*She exits at left with Ella.*

HANNAH (*looks after her*)

Every time I listen to that girl I get fur on my tongue.

JANE

Fur?

HANNAH

Like when my dyspepsia's coming. There's two things I can't abide, her and cucumbers.

[*She crosses to door left.*

JANE

Hannah!

HANNAH (*stops*)

Well?

JANE (*rather shyly*)

We are going to have rather a special supper to-night.

HANNAH (*doubtfully*)

We are?

JANE

Yes. That's why I had you roast that turkey yesterday.

HANNAH (*firmly*)

That's for Sunday!

JANE

No, it's for to-night.

HANNAH (*angrily*)

Why is it?

JANE

It's my birthday.

HANNAH

I did n't know that.

JANE

No, it is n't exactly a national holiday, but we 'll have the turkey, and I 'll get some preserves up, and I want you to bake a cake, a round one. We 'll have candles on it. I got some at the store this morning.

HANNAH (*shocked*)

Candles?

JANE

Yes.

HANNAH

Who 's going to be to this party?

JANE (*a little self-conscious*)

Why — just — just ourselves.

HANNAH

Just you and Mr. Ben and Miss Ella?

JANE

Yes.

HANNAH

You don't want candles on that cake, you want crape on it.

[*She exits door left.*

[*Jane crosses up and starts to clear the dining-room table of its red table cover, as Ben enters door left.*

BEN (*cheerfully*)

Well, I fixed Old Nellie up. (*He puts his bottle back in its place in the wall cabinet*) Just got her in time. Thought she was gone for a minute, but she 's going to be all right.

JANE

That 's good.

[*She folds the tablecloth up and puts it away.*

BEN (*in front of fire*)

She knew what I was doin' for her too; you could
tell by the way she looked at me! She 'll be all right,
poor old critter. I remember her when she was a colt,
year before I went to high school.

[*Jane crosses into room, shutting the dining-room
door after her.*

JANE

You like animals, don't you, Ben?

BEN (*surprised*)

I don't know. I don't like to see 'em suffer.

JANE

Why?

BEN

I guess it 's mostly because they ain't to blame for it.
I mean what comes to 'em ain't their fault. If a
woman thinks she 's sick, 'til she gets sick, that 's
her business. If a man gets drunk, or eats like a hog,
he 's got to pay for it, and he ought to. Animals live
cleaner than we do anyhow — and when you do anything for 'em they 've got gratitude. Folks have n't.

JANE

Hand me that sewing basket, Ben.

[*She has seated herself at left center by table. Ben
at left of table, hands her the basket as she picks up
some sewing.*

BEN

It 's funny, but except for a dog or two, I don't
remember carin' nothin' for any of the live things,
when I lived here I mean.

JANE

I guess that 's because you did n't do much for them.

BEN

I guess so — Sometimes I kind of think I 'd like to be here when spring comes — and see all the young critters coming into the world — I should think there 'd be a lot a feller could do, to make it easier for 'em.

JANE

Yes.

BEN

Everybody 's always makin' a fuss over women and their babies. I guess animals have got some feelings, too.

JANE (*sewing*)

Yes.

BEN

I *know* it — Yes, sometimes I sort of wish I could be here, in the spring.

JANE

You 'll be a big help.

BEN

I 'll be in prison. (*He looks at her. She drops her head and goes on sewing*) You forgot that, did n't yer?

JANE

Yes.

BEN

What 's the difference? A prison ain't just a place; it 's bein' somewheres you don't want to be, and that 's where I 've always been.

JANE

You liked the army?

BEN

I s 'pose so.

JANE

Why?

BEN

I don't know, there was things to do, and you did 'em.

JANE

And some one to tell you what to do?

BEN

Maybe that's it, somebody that knew better 'n I
did. It galled me at first, but pretty soon we got
over in France, an' I saw we was really doin' something, then I did n't mind. I just got to doin' what
I was told, and it worked out all right.

JANE

You liked France, too?

BEN

Yes.

JANE

I'd like to hear you tell about it.

BEN

Maybe I'll go back there some time. I don't know
as I'd mind farming a place over there. Most of
their farms are awful little, but I don't know but
what I'd like it.

JANE

Farming is farming. Why not try it here?

BEN

Look out there! (*He points out of the window at
the drifted snow*) It's like that half the year, froze
up, everything, most of all the people. Just a
family by itself, maybe. Just a few folks, good an'
bad, month after month, with nothin' to think about
but just the mean little things, that really don't

amount to nothin', but get to be bigger than all the world outside.

JANE (*sewing*)

Somebody must do the farming, Ben.

BEN

Somebody like the Jordans, that's been doin' it generation after generation. Well, look at us. I heard a feller, in a Y.M.C.A. hut, tellin' how nature brought animals into the world, able to face what they had to face ——

JANE

Yes, Ben?

BEN

That's what nature's done for us Jordans, — brought us into the world half froze before we was born. Brought us into the world mean, and hard, so 's we could live the hard, mean life we have to live.

JANE

I don't know, Ben, but what you could live it different.

BEN

They *laugh* over there, and sing, and God knows when I was there they did n't have much to sing about. I was at a rest camp, near Nancy, after I got wounded. I told you about the French lady with all those children that I got billeted with.

JANE

Yes.

BEN

They used to *sing*, right at the table, and laugh! God! It brought a lump into my throat mor'n once, lookin' at them, and rememberin' the Jordans!

JANE

I guess there was n't much laughing at your family table.

BEN

Summers nobody had much time for it, and winters, — well, I guess you know.

JANE

Yes.

BEN

Just a few folks together, day after day, and every little thing you don't like about the other raspin' on your nerves 'til it almost drives you crazy! Most folks quiet, because they 've said all the things they 've got to say a hundred times; other folks talkin', talkin', talkin' about nothing. Sometimes somebody sort of laughs, and it scares you; seems like laughter needs the sun, same as flowers do. Icebound, that 's what we are all of us, inside and out.

[*He stands looking grimly out window.*

JANE

Not all.   I laughed a lot before I came here to live.

BEN (*turns and looks at her*)

I remember, you were just a little girl.

JANE

I was fourteen.   See if there 's a spool of black sewing cotton in that drawer.

BEN (*looking in drawer*)

You mean thread?

JANE

Yes.

BEN

This it?

[*He holds up a spool of white thread.*

JANE

Would you call that black?

BEN (*looks it over*)

No — it ain't black. (*He searches and finds black thread*) Maybe this is it!

JANE

Maybe it is! (*She takes it*) You were with that French family quite a while, were n't you?

BEN

Most a month; they was well off, you know; I mean, they was, before the war. It was a nice house.

JANE (*sewing*)

How nice?

BEN (*hesitates*)

I don't know, things — well — useful, you know, but nice, not like this.

[*He looks about.*

JANE (*looks around with a sigh*)

It 's not very pretty, but it could be. I could make it.

BEN

If you did, folks would be sayin' you was n't respectable.

JANE

Tell me about the dinner they gave you the night before you went back to your company.

BEN

I told you.

JANE

Tell me again.

BEN (*smiles to himself at the remembrance*)

They was all dressed up, the whole family, and there I was with just my dirty old uniform.

JANE

Yes.

BEN (*lost in his recollections*)

It was a fine dinner, but it wasn't that. It was their doin' so much for me, folks like that — I 've sort of pictured 'em lots of times since then.

JANE

Go on.

BEN

All of the young ones laughing and happy, and the mother too, laughing and tryin' to talk to me, and neither one of us knowing much about what the other one was sayin'.

[*He and Jane both laugh.*

JANE

And the oldest daughter? The one that was most grown up?

BEN

She was scared of me somehow, but I don't know as ever I 've seen a girl like her, before or since.

JANE

Maybe 'twas that dress you told me about; seems to me you don't remember much else about her; not so much as what color her hair was, only just that that dress was blue.

BEN (*thoughtfully*)

Yes.

JANE (*sewing*)

Sometimes you say dark blue!

[*She is watching him closely through half-shut eyes.*

BEN (*absently*)

I guess so.

JANE

And then I say, dark as something I point out to you, that isn't dark at all, and you say, "No, lighter than that!"

BEN (*absently*)

Just — sort of blue.

JANE

Yes, sort of blue. It had lace on it, too, didn't it?

BEN

Lace? Maybe — yes, lace.

JANE

There's more than one blue dress in the world.

BEN

Like enough. Maybe there's mor'n one family like that lady's, but I'll be damned if they live in Veazie. (*He crosses and opens cupboard and selects a bottle*) I might as well run out and see how the old mare is getting on.

[*He selects bottle from shelf.*

JANE

And you've got to shovel those paths for the clothes lines yet.

BEN

I know.

JANE

Well, don't forget.

BEN

It ain't likely you'll let me.

[*He exits at door right. Jane laughs softly to herself, and runs to closet and takes out a large cardboard box and putting it on the table, she cuts the*

*string and removes the wrapping paper, then lifts
the cover of the box and draws out a dainty light-
blue gown with soft lace on the neck and sleeves. She
holds it up joyfully, then covering her own dress
with it, she looks at herself in a mirror on wall. As
she stands smiling at her reflection, there is a sharp
knock on the outside door. Jane hastily returns dress
to box and as the knock is repeated, she puts the box
under the sofa at left and crosses and opens the outside door.*

Judge Bradford enters.

JANE

Oh, it's you, Judge! Come in.

JUDGE

I thought I'd stop on my way home and see how
you were getting on, Jane.

JANE

I'll take your coat.

JUDGE

I'll just put it here. (*He puts coat on chair*)
Have you time to sit down a minute?

JANE

Of course.

[*They sit.*

JUDGE (*looks at her*)

That is n't a smile on your lips, is it, Jane?

JANE

Maybe ——

JUDGE (*laughingly*)

I'm glad I came!

JANE

It's my birthday.

JUDGE

Why, Jane! (*He crosses to her and holds out his hand. She takes it*) Many happy returns!

JANE (*thoughtfully*)

Many — happy returns — that's a lot to ask for.

JUDGE

You're about twenty-two, or twenty-three, are n't you?

JANE

Twenty-three.

JUDGE

Time enough ahead of you. (*His eye falls on the box, imperfectly hidden under the sofa; out of it a bit of the blue dress is sticking*) Hello! What's all that?

JANE

My birthday present.

JUDGE

Who gave it to you?

JANE

I did.

JUDGE

Good! It's about time you started to blossom out.

JANE

I ordered a lot of things from Boston; they'll be here to-morrow.

JUDGE

I suppose that one's a dress?

JANE

Yes.

JUDGE (*bends over to look*)

Light blue, is n't it?

JANE (*smiles*)

Just sort of blue — with lace on it.

JUDGE

Oh, you 're going to wear it, I suppose, in honor of your birthday?

JANE (*startled*)

To-night — oh, no — soon maybe, but not to-night.

JUDGE (*smiles*)

How soon?

JANE

Soon as I dare to; not just yet.

JUDGE

You have plenty of money; you ought to have every comfort in the world, and some of the luxuries.

JANE (*gravely*)

Judge! I want you to do something for me.

JUDGE

And of course I 'll do it.

JANE

I want you to get Ben off. I want you to fix it so he won't go to State's Prison.

JUDGE

But if he 's guilty, Jane?

JANE

I want you to go to old Mr. Kimbal for me and offer to pay him for that barn of his that Ben burned down. Then I want you to fix it so he won't push the case, so 's Ben gets off.

JUDGE

Do you know what you are asking of me?

JANE

To get Ben off.

JUDGE

　To compound a felony.

JANE

　Those are just words, Judge, and words don't matter much to me. I might say I was n't asking you to compound a felony. I was askin' you to save a sinner, but those would be just words too. There's nobody else; you 've *got* to help me.

JUDGE (*thoughtfully*)

　I 've always thought a lot could be done for Ben, by a good lawyer.

JANE

　It does n't matter how, so long as it 's done.

JUDGE

　He was drinking, with a crowd of young men; the two Kimbal boys jumped on him and beat him up rather badly. That 's about all we know, aside from the fact that Ben was drunk, and that that night the Kimbals' barn was set on fire.

JANE

　Just so long as you can get him off, Judge.

JUDGE

　I think a case of assault could be made against the Kimbal boys, and I think it would stand.

JANE

　What of it?

JUDGE

　It is quite possible that the old man, if he knew that action was to be taken against his sons, and if he could be tactfully assured of payment for his barn, say by Ben, in a year's time, might be persuaded to petition to have the indictment against Ben withdrawn. In that event, I think the chances would be very much in Ben's favor.

JANE

I don't care what names you call it, so long as it's done. Will you fix it?

JUDGE

Well, it's not exactly a proper proceeding for a Judge of the Circuit Court.

JANE

I knew you'd do it.

JUDGE

Yes, and I think you knew why, did n't you?

JANE

Ever since she's died, you've helped me about everything. Before she died you were just as good to me, and nobody else was.

JUDGE

I am glad you said that, because it clears me from the charge of being what poor Ben calls " one of the crow buzzards," and I don't want you to think me that.

JANE

No, you're not that.

JUDGE

I love you, Jane.

JANE

No!

JUDGE

Yes — I've done that for a long while. Don't you think you could get used to the thought of being my wife?

JANE (*gently*)

No.

JUDGE

I think I could make you happy.

JANE

No.

JUDGE

I am afraid being happy is something you don't know very much about.

JANE

No.

JUDGE

It is n't a thing that I am going to hurry you over, my dear, but neither is it a thing that I am going to give up hoping for.

JANE

When you told me, that day, that Mrs. Jordan had left me all her money, I could n't understand; then, afterwards, you gave me the letter she left for me. I want you to read it.

JUDGE

What has her letter to do with us?

JANE

Maybe, reading it, you 'll get to know something you 've got a right to know, better than I could tell it to you.

JUDGE

Very well.

JANE

It 's here. (*She opens drawer, and selects a letter in a woman's old-fashioned handwriting, from a large envelope of papers*) She was a cold woman, Judge. She never let me get close to her, although I tried. She did n't love me. I was as sure of it then as I am now. (*She holds out the letter*) Read it.

JUDGE

If it's about the thing I've been speaking of, I'd
rather hear it in your voice.

JANE (*reads*)

"My dear Jane, the doctor tells me I have n't long to
live, and so I'm doing this, the meanest thing I think
I've ever done to you. I'm leaving you the Jordan
money. Since my husband died, there has been just
one person I could get to care about; that's Ben,
who was my baby so long after all the others had
forgotten how to love me. And Ben's a bad son,
and a bad man. I can't leave him the money; he'd
squander it, and the Jordans' money came hard."

JUDGE

Poor woman! It was a bitter thing for her to have
to write like that.

JANE (*reads on*)

"If squandering the money would bring him happi-
ness, I'd face all the Jordans in the other world and
laugh at them, but I know there's only just one
chance to save my boy, — through a woman who will
hold out her heart to him and let him trample on it,
as he has on mine."

JUDGE (*in sudden fear*)

Jane!

JANE (*reads on*)

"Who'd work, and pray, and live for him, until as
age comes on, and maybe he gets a little tired, he'll
turn to her. And you're that woman, Jane; you've
loved him ever since you came to us. Although he
does n't even know it. The Jordan name is his, the
money's yours, and maybe there'll be another life
for you to guard. God knows it is n't much I'm

leaving you, but you can't refuse it, because you love him, and when he knows the money is yours, he will want to marry you. I 'm a wicked old woman. Maybe you 'll learn to forgive me as time goes on — It takes a long time to make a Jordan." (*Jane drops her hand to her side*) Then she just signed her name.

JUDGE

Is the damnable thing she says there true?

JANE

Yes, Judge.

JUDGE

And you 're going to do this thing for her?

JANE

No, for him.

JUDGE (*bitterly*)

He is n't worth it.

JANE

I guess you don't understand.

JUDGE

No.

[*He crosses and picks up his coat.*

JANE

You can't go like that, angry. You have to pay a price for being a good man, Judge — I need your help.

JUDGE

You mean *he* needs my help?

JANE

Yes, and you 'll have to give it to him, if what you said a little while ago was true.

JUDGE (*after a pause*)

   It *was* true, Jane. I 'll help him.

   [*He picks up his hat.*

JANE

   I 've an errand at the store. I 'll go with you.

   [*She takes hat and coat from rack and puts them on.*

JUDGE

   Is it anything I could have sent up for you?

JANE (*putting on coat*)

   I guess not. You see, I 've got to match a color.

JUDGE

   Another new dress?

JANE (*they start toward door*)

   Just a ribbon, for my hair.

JUDGE

   I did n't know women still wore ribbons in their hair.

JANE

   It seems they do — in France.

   . . [*They exit together at left to the outside door and off.*

   Nettie and Ella enter quickly, after a slight pause, Nettie running in from right, followed more sedately by Ella.

NETTIE

   You see! I was right! She went with him.

   [*She has run to window left and is looking out.*

ELLA

   That 's what money does. If mother had n't left her everything, he would n't have touched her with a ten-foot pole.

NETTIE

   Well, if she 's fool enough to stay in this place, I guess he 's about the best there is.

ELLA

Then trust her for gettin' him; by the time she gets through in Veazie, this town will be barer than Mother Hubbard's cupboard by the time the dog got there. (*Her eye falls on Jane's box, partly under sofa.*) What's that?
[*She bends over, looking at it.*

NETTIE

What?

ELLA

I never saw it before. (*She draws it out*) Looks like a dress. See! Blue silk!

NETTIE

Open it.

ELLA (*hesitates*)

Must be hers! Maybe she would n't like it.

NETTIE

Maybe she would n't know it.

ELLA

A cat can look at a king!
[*She opens the box and holds up the blue dress.*

NETTIE

Oh! Oh!

ELLA (*really moved*)

Some folks would say a dress like that was n't decent, but I would n't care, not if it was mine, and it might have been mine — but for her.

NETTIE

Yours! Grandma would n't have left her money to you. She hated old people. Everybody does. She 'd have left it to me, but for Jane Crosby!

ELLA (*looks at dress*)

I always wanted a dress like this; when I was young, I used to dream about one, but mother only laughed. For years I counted on gettin' me what I wanted, when she died; now I never will.

NETTIE (*fiercely*)

I will — somehow!

ELLA

Maybe but not me. Oh, if I could have the feelin' of a dress like that on me, if I could wear it once, where folks could see me — Just once! Oh, I know how they 'd laugh — I would n't care ——

NETTIE (*almost in tears*)

I can't stand it if she 's going to wear things like that.

ELLA

I 'll put it back.
[*She starts to do so.*

NETTIE (*catches her hand*)

Not yet.

ELLA

I guess the less we look at it, the better off we 'll be.
[*There is a ring at the front door.*

NETTIE

Who 's that?

ELLA

Here! (*She hands the box to Nettie*) Shove it back under the sofa. I 'll go and see. (*She turns and crosses to door left and out to the vestibule. Nettie, with the box in her arms, hesitates for a moment then turns and exits at right, taking the box with her.*

*Ella opens the outside door at left, showing Orin
on the doorstep. Ella looks at him angrily)* For
time's sake, what are *you* ringing the bell for?

ORIN

Mum says for me not to act like I belonged here.

ELLA

Well, I'm goin' to shut the door. Git in or git out!

ORIN

I got a note. (*He enters room as Ella shuts door*)
It's for her.

ELLA (*holds out hand*)

Let me see it.

ORIN

Mum said not to let on I had nothin' if you came
nosin' around.

[*Jane enters from left.*

JANE

I just ran across to the store. I haven't been five
minutes.

[*She takes coat off.*

ELLA

He's got a note for you, from Sadie.

JANE

Oh, let me see it, Orin.

ORIN (*gives her note*)

She said, if you said is they an answer, I was to say
yes, they is.

JANE

Just a minute.

[*She opens note and reads it.*

ELLA

I must say she did n't lose much time.

JANE (*after reading note*)　Poor Sadie!　Wait, Orin!
(*She sits at table and takes checkbook from the
drawer and writes*)　Just take this to your mother.

ELLA

You don't mean you 're goin' to ——

JANE

Be quiet, Ella.　Here, Orin.　(*She hands him check*)
Don't lose it, and run along.

ORIN

All right.　Mum said we was goin' to have dinner
early, and go to a movie!　Good night.

JANE (*again writing in checkbook*)

Good night.
[*Orin exits.*

ELLA

So you sent her her rent money, after all?

JANE

Here!
[*She rises and hands a check to Ella.*

ELLA

What 's that?

JANE

Two hundred dollars.　You can try that dressmaking
business if you want to, Ella.

ELLA

[*Looks at check.*
Two hundred dollars!

JANE

You need n't thank me.

ELLA

That ain't it.　I was just wonderin' what 's come
over you all of a sudden.
[*Ben enters,*

JANE

It 's my birthday, that 's all.   Did you know it was my birthday, Ben?

BEN (*carelessly*)

Is it?   I shoveled them damned paths !

[*He crosses and sits by fire.*

JANE

Ella 's going into the dressmaking business, Ben.

BEN (*moodily*)

What of it?

ELLA

That 's what I say.   It ain't much of a business.

[*She exits at right; outside it grows to dusk.*

JANE

Are you tired?

BEN

Maybe.

[*He stretches his feet out toward fire.*

JANE

You 've done a lot of work to-day.

BEN

And every day.

JANE

I don't suppose you know how much good it 's done you, how well you look !

BEN

Beauty 's only skin deep.

JANE

Folks change, even in a few weeks, outside and in. Hard work don't hurt anybody.

BEN

I got chilblains on my feet.   The damned shoes are stiffer than they ever was.

JANE

Icebound, you said. Maybe it don't have to be like that. Sometimes, just lately, it's seemed to me that if folks would try, things need n't be so bad. All of 'em try, I mean, for themselves, and for everybody else.

BEN

If I was you, I'd go out somewheres and hire a hall.

JANE

If you'd put some pork fat on those shoes to-night, your feet would n't hurt so bad.

BEN

Maybe.

[*He sits looking moodily into the fire. After a moment's hesitation, Jane crosses and sits in the chair beside his, the evening shadows deepen around them but the glow from the fire lights their faces.*

JANE

I'm lonesome to-night. We always made a lot of birthdays when I was a girl.

BEN

Some do.

JANE

Your mother did n't. She found me once trying, the day I was fifteen. I remember how she laughed at me.

BEN

All the Jordans have got a sense of humor.

JANE

She was n't a Jordan, not until she married your father.

BEN

When a woman marries into a family, she mostly shuts her eyes and jumps in all over.

JANE

Your mother was the best of the whole lot of you. Anyway, I think so.

BEN

I *know* it. I always thought a lot of her, in spite of our being relations.

JANE

She loved you, Ben.

BEN

She left me without a dollar, knowin' I was going to State's Prison, and what I 'd be by the time I get out.

JANE

Maybe some day you 'll understand why she did it.

BEN

Because she thought you 'd take better care of the money than any of the rest of us.

JANE

And you hate me because of that, the way all the rest of the Jordans do?

BEN

Sometimes.

JANE (*sadly*)

I suppose it 's natural.

BEN

But I ain't such a fool as Henry, and the women folks. They think you took advantage and fooled her into what she did. I thought so at first, now I don't.

JANE

What do you think now, Ben?

BEN

She 'd watched you; she knew you were worth mor'n all of us in a lump. I know it, too, but some way it riles me worse than if you was n't.

JANE

That 's silly!

BEN (*with growing resentment*)

Don't you suppose I know what you 've been doin' to me. Tryin' to make a man of me. Tryin' to help me. Standing up to me and fightin' me every day, tryin' to teach me to be decent. Workin' over me like I was a baby, or somethin', and you was tryin' to teach me how to walk. Gettin' me so upset that every time I don't do what I ought to do, I get all het up inside; I never was so damned uncomfortable in all my life.

JANE

And I never was so happy.

BEN

I s 'pose God knew what he was about when he made women.

JANE

Of course he did.

BEN

Anyhow, he gave 'em the best of it, all right.

JANE

You don't mean that! You *can't!*

BEN

I do. Let a man get miserable, and he *is* miserable. A woman ain't really happy no other way.

JANE

Maybe you think I 'm having an easier time right now than you are.

BEN

I know it.

JANE

They all hate me, and they all want something, all the time. I can't say yes, and it's hard to always say no. Then there's the farm, big, and poor, and all worked out. The Jordans have been taking their living out of this soil for more than a hundred years, and never putting anything back.

BEN

Just themselves, that's all.

JANE

Worked right, like they do out West, this place could be what it ought to be. How can I do that; it needs a man.

BEN

I been thinkin' lately things could be done a whole lot different.

JANE

By a man, if he loved the old place — You Jordans robbed this soil always. Suppose one of you tried to pay it back — it would mean work and money, for a couple of years maybe, then I guess you'd see what gratitude meant.

BEN

It could be done; it ought to be.

JANE

By you, Ben!

BEN

No — I guess I ain't got the judgment.

JANE

You've got it, if you'd learn to use it.

BEN

Anyhow, I 've got just a month, that 's all.

JANE

Maybe you 'll have more.

BEN

I 'm as good as convicted as I sit here. I 've only got a month.

JANE

Then help me for that month. We could plan how to start out in the spring. I 've got books that will help us, and I can get more. We could do a lot!

BEN

I don't know but what we could!

JANE (*bends toward him*)

Will you shake hands on it?
[*She offers her hand.*

BEN (*surprised*)

What for?

JANE

Oh, just because we never have.

BEN

We ain't goin' to change *everything*, are we?

JANE

One thing. We 're going to be friends.

BEN (*takes her hand awkwardly*)

You 're a good sport, game as a man, gamer maybe.

JANE

And now for the surprise.

BEN

The what!

JANE (*draws her hand away and rises*)

You 'll see.   I want you to sit right here, until I open those doors.

[*She points to doors to dining room.*

BEN

I was n't thinkin' of movin'.

JANE

Just sit right there.

BEN

And do what?

JANE

Think.

BEN

What of?

JANE

Oh, anything — so long as it 's pleasant — of the spring that 's coming ——

BEN

In the prison down at Thomaston.

JANE

Of France then, of the family that was so good to you — of the beautiful lady — of the daughter, if you want to, the one that was most grown up — and of the wonderful blue dress.   Just shut your eyes and think, 'til I come back!

[*She exits through doors to dining room and closes the doors after her.   Ben sits in glow from the fire, his eyes closed.   In a moment the door at right is thrown open and Nettie stands in the doorway, the light from the hall falling on her.   She has on Jane's blue dress and is radiant with youth and excitement.*

NETTIE

Ben!   Look at me!   Look, Ben!

BEN

What?

NETTIE

Look Ben!

[*He looks at her and for a moment sits in stupid wonder, then rises slowly to his feet.*

BEN

It 's — It 's Nettie!

NETTIE

Did you ever see anything so lovely, did you?

BEN

You 're — you 're a woman, Nettie!

NETTIE

Of course I am, you stupid!

BEN (*crosses down to her*)

God! How I 've starved for somethin' pretty to look at! God! How I 've starved for it!

NETTIE

That 's why I came down, I wanted you to see! I waited there in the hall till she went out.

BEN

And you 've been here all the time, and I have n't so much as looked at you!

NETTIE (*softly*)

You 've been in trouble, Ben!

BEN

I 'll get out of that somehow! I 'm going to make a fight. I ain't goin' to let 'em take me now.

NETTIE

Honest, Ben?

BEN

  Not now.　Oh, you pretty kid!　You pretty little
thing!

  [*He catches her fiercely in his arms.*

NETTIE

  You must n't, Ben!

BEN (*triumphant*)

  Must n't!　You don't know me!

NETTIE

  Just one then!　(*She holds up her lips, and as he
kisses her ardently, the dining-room doors back of
them open and Jane stands in the doorway, looking
at them.　She has removed her apron and has made
some poor attempt at dressing up.　Back of her we
see the table bravely spread for the festive birthday
party.　There is a large turkey and other special
dishes, and a round cake on which blaze twenty-two
tiny candles.　They turn their heads, startled, as
Jane looks at them, and Ben tightens his arms defi-
antly about Nettie*)　Let me go!

BEN (*holding her and looking past her to Jane*)　No!
(*Then to Jane*)　Why are you looking at me like
that?

NETTIE

  Let me go.

BEN (*to Jane*)

  To hell with your dream of grubbing in the dirt.
Now I know what I want, and I 'm going to get it.

NETTIE

  Let go, dear.　(*She draws away*)　I 'm ashamed
about wearin' your dress, Cousin Jane.　I 'll take it
right off.

JANE

    You need n't. I guess I don't want it any more. (*For the first time her eyes leave Ben's face. She turns and steps past them to the door at right and calls*) Supper 's ready, Ella!

[*Hannah enters at back in dining room with a plate of hot biscuits.*

CURTAIN

ACT III

Scene: Same as Act One. Parlor at the Jordans',
two months later.

At rise the characters are grouped exactly as they
were at the opening of the play. The white slip covers,
however, have been removed from the chairs, and the
backing through the window shows partly melted snow
drifts. Henry sighs; the clock strikes two. Henry
looks at his watch.

There is a pause. The outside door slams and Ben
enters and looks about.

BEN
Well — here we all are again.

SADIE (*sadly*)
Yes.

HENRY
I ain't been in this room before since the funeral.

SADIE
And I ain't, and the last time before that was when
father died.

EMMA
I sat right here, in the same chair I'm settin' in now,
but to your grandfather's funeral, right after I
married Henry, I was treated like one of the poor
relations! I had to stand up.

HENRY
I remember; it made considerable trouble.

ELLA

I don't know as it was ever what I called a cheerful room.

HENRY (*severely*)

A parlor's where a person's supposed to sit and think of God, and you couldn't expect it to be cheerful!

ELLA (*looks about*)

Seems like we'd had trouble and disgrace enough in this family without her takin' all the slip covers off of the chairs and sofa!

EMMA

It ain't *right!*

SADIE

That Boston woman that's building the house over on Elm Street ain't so much as goin' to have a parlor. I stopped her right on the street and asked her what she was plannin' to do soon as the first of 'em died.

EMMA

What did she say?

SADIE

Said she tried not to think about such things.

HENRY (*sternly*)

We got Atheists enough in this town right now.

BEN

Well, if Jane's coming I wish she'd come; this ain't exactly my idea of pleasant company.

ELLA

She says we're all to wait in here for Judge Bradford.

SADIE

What did she send for us for?

ELLA

I don't know.

EMMA

Why did n't you ask her?

ELLA

I did, and she most bit my head off.

BEN

She most bites mine off every time I see her. I must say she 's changed, Jane has; she ain't the same girl at all she was a few weeks ago.

NETTIE

She 's actin' just awful, especially to me!

SADIE

Of course, I 'd be the last one to say anything against her, but ——

BEN

But nothin'! There ain't one of you here fit to tie her shoes!

SADIE

We ain't?

BEN

And I ain't! The only difference between us is I ain't worth much and I know it, and you ain't worth nothin' and you don't.

EMMA

I guess you 'd better be careful how you talk!

NETTIE

If anybody says anything about Jane lately, that 's the way he always talks! The worse she treats him the better he seems to like it,

SADIE

Well, I don't know as I 'm surprised more about his insultin' the rest of us, but it 's sort of comical his talkin' that way about you, Nettie.

EMMA

Nettie! What 's Nettie got to do with him?

SADIE

Oh! Excuse me! I did n't know 't was supposed to be a secret.

EMMA

What is?

SADIE

About the way those two have been carryin' on together!

HENRY

What!

ELLA

Ben and Nettie!

NETTIE (*afraid*)

Stop her, Ben, can't you?

BEN

If I knew a way to stop women like her I 'd patent it and get rich!

EMMA (*sternly*)

Him and Nettie?

SADIE

They passed my house together *once* a week ago Wednesday, *once* the Tuesday before that, and *twice* the Sunday after New Year's.

HENRY

Together!

SADIE

And Eben Tilden's boy told Abbie Palsey that Tilly Hickson heard Aaron Hamlin say he'd seen 'em together at the picture show!

HENRY (*to Ben*)

Is it true?

EMMA

You've been with him after all I told you!

BEN

It ain't going to hurt her none just to talk to me, is it?

EMMA

Them that touches pitch gets defiled!

HENRY (*to Nettie*)

I want you to tell me everything that's took place between you two.

SADIE

Wait!

HENRY

What?

SADIE

Orin! Leave the room!

NETTIE

He don't have to leave the room. I don't care who knows what happened!

HENRY

Go on then.

NETTIE

Well — Ben and I — We — Just for a few days — anyway, it was all his fault.

BEN

She threw me down because I was going to prison.

NETTIE

He said he 'd get out of it somehow, but he can't, and I just won't have folks laughing at me!

BEN

It 's all right, it never meant nothin' to her, and I guess it did n't mean much to me. It 's just as well it 's over.

NETTIE

It 's a whole lot better.

HENRY

Well — what 's passed is passed. Folks that plant the wind reap the whirlwind! There 's no use cryin' over spilled milk.

ORIN

Say, Mum! What do you s 'pose Uncle Henry thinks he means when he says things?

HENRY

Somehow I can't help wishin' you was my son for just about five minutes.

[*Hannah and Judge Bradford enter.*

HANNAH

They 're all in here, Judge.

JUDGE

Good afternoon.

HENRY

How are you, Judge?

SADIE

It 's a mild day; winter 's most over. Stop scratching yourself.

[*This last to Orin who seems to be uneasy and frequently scratches himself.*

HANNAH (*at door*)
I 'll tell her you 're here, Judge. She 'll be right
down.
[*Hannah exits.*

ELLA
Won't you sit?

JUDGE
Thanks.
[*He sits by table.*

HENRY
What 's it about? Why did she say we was to all be
here at two o'clock?

JUDGE
She will probably be able to answer that question
herself, Ben.

SADIE (*to Orin*)
Don't.

ORIN
What?

SADIE
Scratch!

ORIN
Oh.
[*Jane enters. The Judge rises.*

JUDGE
Well, Jane?

JANE
Don't get up, Judge.

JUDGE
Will you sit here?
[*Judge turns to get a chair for Jane. Orin scratches
himself. Ella rises.*

ELLA

What is the matter with this brat?

ORIN

I itch!

SADIE

It's warm, and he's got on his heavy flannels! He's as clean as you are!
[*Jane and Judge sit.*

BEN

You said to heat this room up and wait here for you and the Judge. Why? I got my stock to tend.

HENRY

It's a bad time for me to get away from the store; What was it you wanted of us?

JANE

I'm afraid it isn't going to be easy to tell you.

JUDGE

Won't you let me do it, Jane?

JANE

No. I've come to know that your mother didn't really want that I should have the Jordan money.

SADIE

What's that?

JANE

I put it as simply as I could.

BEN

You mean a later will's been found?

JUDGE

No.

JANE

In a way, Judge, it's like there had. Your mother left me a letter dated later than the will.

ELLA

Leavin' the money different?

JANE

Tellin' what she really wanted.

BEN

Well, what did she want?

JANE

It was like she left me all her money in trust, so I
could keep it safe until the time she was hopin' for
come, and in a way it did come, not quite like she
wanted it, but near enough so I can give up a burden
I have n't strength enough to carry any more.
[*She stops.*

JUDGE

Let me finish, Jane.   Jane has asked me to draw a
deed of gift, making the Jordan property over to
Ben.

BEN

Why?

JANE

She wanted you to have it.

BEN

Why did n't she will it to me, then?

JANE

She was afraid to trust you.

BEN

Well?

JANE

You 've learned to work; you 'll keep on working.

HENRY

You mean to say my mother wanted him to have it
all?

JANE

Yes.

HENRY

I am a religious man, but there was a time when even Job gave up! So — all our money goes to Ben — and he can't even buy himself out of prison!

JANE (*after a pause*)

Ben is n't going to prison.

BEN

Why? Who's to stop it?

JUDGE (*after a look from Jane*)

Kimbal agreed not to press the charge against you. It seems that there were certain extenuating circumstances. A motion has been made for the dismissal of the indictment, and it won't be opposed.

BEN

Why did he? Who fixed this thing.

JANE

Judge Bradford did.

[*She looks at Judge.*

BEN (*slowly*)

It means a lot to me. There's things I'd like to do. I have n't dared to think about 'em lately — now I'll do 'em.

[*There is a pause.*

HENRY

Well, Ben, so you've got the money! I guess maybe it's better than her havin' it; after all blood's thicker than water! We'll help you any way we can and — er — of course you'll help us.

BEN

Why will I?

HENRY

　We're brothers, Ben! We're old Jordans!

BEN

　What was we when I got back from France? There was a band met us boys at the station. I was your brother all right that day, only somehow, in just a little while you forgot about it. I was a Jordan when I was hidin' out from the police, and all that kept me from starvin' was the money Jane sent me! I was your brother the night mother died, and you said you would n't go my bail.

ELLA

　You ain't going to be hard, Ben!

BEN

　I'm the head of the family now, ain't I, and you can bet all you've got I'm going to be a real Jordan.

HENRY

　I think, Ben ——

BEN

　From now on, there ain't nobody got any right to think in this house but just me! So run along home, the whole pack of you, and after this, when you feel like you must come here — come separate.

ELLA

　Turn us out, Ben?

BEN

　Sure, why not?

NETTIE (*crosses to him. Sweetly*)

　There ain't any reason why *we* can't be friends, is there?

BEN

　Well, I don't know. There's only one way I could ever get to trust you.

NETTIE

What way, Ben?

BEN

I'd have to go to jail for five years and see if you'd
wait for me!

EMMA

It's an awful thing for a mother to have a fool for
a child.

ELLA (*goes upstage with Nettie*)

Well, I must say you made a nice mess of things!

NETTIE (*exits with Ella*)

Well, I don't care! I don't see how anybody would
expect me to be a mind reader!

SADIE

Come, Orin — say good-by to your Uncle Ben.

ORIN

What will I do that for?

SADIE

Because I tell you to!

ORIN

Yesterday you told me he was n't worth speakin' to!

SADIE

Are you going to move, you stupid little idiot.

[*She drags him out.*

ORIN (*as they go*)

What did I say? You let me alone!

HENRY

I was wonderin', Ben, how you'd feel about endorsing that note of mine.

BEN

You was?

HENRY

Yes, I don't know what I'm going to do about it.

BEN

As far as I care, you can go nail it on a door. (*Henry and Emma start to exit*) No, hold on, I'll pay it.

HENRY

You will!

BEN

Yes, I don't know as it would do me much good at the bank, havin' a brother of mine in the poorhouse. [*Ben laughs as Henry and Emma exit.*

JUDGE

Well, Ben? "Uneasy lies the head that wears a crown."

BEN (*down to stove*)

Depends on the head. Mine's thick, I guess. Anyhow, none of them is going to bother it. I'm boss here now.

JUDGE

You'll find a copy here of the inventory of the estate, and other legal papers. Everything is in order.

JANE

And my accounts, Ben; you'll find the exact amount your mother left. I spent some money about six weeks ago, on myself, but I've been careful ever since and I've made up for it.

BEN

You said, Judge, she did n't have to go by that letter of my mother's, if she did n't want to? She did n't have to give anything back at all?

JUDGE

No, she did n't.

BEN

Then if I was you — (*to Jane*) I would n't

much about the little you spent on yourself. I guess
to look at you it was n't much.

JANE

Yes, it was.

BEN

Well, we 'll fix things so you can keep on spendin'.
Only let 's see somethin' come of it. I never was so
damned sick of anything in my life as I am of that
old black dress of yours!

[*Crosses stage up and over right.*

JANE

I 've got plenty of clothes upstairs. I 'm sorry now
I ever bought them, but I 'll take them with me when
I go.

BEN

Go? Go where?

JANE

To Old Town. I 've got a place there, clerking in the
Pulp Mill.

BEN

You!

JANE

Yes.

BEN

But what about me?

JUDGE

Don't you think Jane has done about enough for
you?

BEN

She 's done a lot, she 's given up the money. I don't
know as I like that; 'course I like gettin' it, but not if
she 's going away.

JANE

I could n't stay now, and I would n't want to.

BEN

I don't suppose you remember about plannin' what you and me was to do with this old farm?

JANE

I remember.

BEN

Well — then what are you going away for?

JANE

Because I could n't be happy here, Ben — It 's been harder than anything I ever thought could come to anybody, the last few weeks here — and so I 'm going. (*She turns to Judge*) I 'll go upstairs and get my things. I 'll stop at your office, Judge, on the way to the station.

JUDGE

Thank you, Jane.

BEN

You 're goin' to-day? Before I order my new farm machinery or anything? You 're goin' to leave me with all this work on my hands?

JANE

Yes, Ben.
[*She exits.*

BEN

Well — that 's a lesson to me! Oh, she 's a good woman! I ain't denyin' that — but she 's fickle!

JUDGE

You 're a fool, Ben!

BEN

I been doin' kitchen police around this town for quite a spell now, Judge, but from this day on I ain't goin' to take that sort of talk from anybody.

JUDGE

I assure you that you won't have to take any sort of talk at all from me.

[*He starts for the door.*

BEN

I did n't mean that. I don't want you to think I ain't grateful for all you 've done for me.

JUDGE (*coldly*)

I have done nothing for you.

BEN

If it was n't for you, I 'd want to die; that 's what I did want. I was afraid of that prison, just a coward about it. Now I 'm a free man, with a big life openin' out ahead of me — I got everything in the world right here in my two hands, everything — and I owe it to you!

JUDGE

I am very glad to say that you don't owe me anything. I don't like you, I have n't forgiven you for what you did to your mother's life. Nor for a worse thing, one you have n't brains enough to even know you 've done. Don't be grateful to me, Ben, please. I think nothing could distress me more than that.

BEN

You 've been a good friend to me.

JUDGE

I have n't meant to be, as I said I don't like you. I have n't any faith in you. I don't believe in this new life of yours. You made a mess of the old one, and I think you will of the new.

BEN

No matter what you say, you can't get away from me. I'll be grateful till I die. But for you I'd have gone to that damned prison!

JUDGE

But for Jane.

BEN

How Jane?

JUDGE

How Jane? Jane went your bond the day your mother died. Jane took you in and taught you how to work, made you work, taught you through the one decent spot in you something of a thing you'd never know, self-respect. Worked over you, petted you, coaxed you — held you up — Then you hurt her — but she kept on — She went herself to Kimbal, after he had refused me, and got his help to keep you out of prison — then, against my will, against the best that I could do to stop her, she turns over all this to you — and goes out with nothing — and you ask " How Jane? "

BEN

Why? Why has she done this, all this, for me?
[*The Judge looks at Ben with contempt and turns and exits. Ben is left in deep thought. Jane comes downstairs dressed for a journey with a hand bag, etc. She enters.*

JANE

Good-by, Ben. (*She crosses to him, her hand out*)
Good-by. Won't you say good-by?

BEN

First, there's some things I got to know about.

JANE (*smiles*)

I guess there's not much left for us to say, Ben.

BEN (*she crosses to door, but he gets ahead of her*)
There's things I got to know. (*She looks at him but does not speak*) The Judge tells me 't was you got Kimbal to let me go free. (*He looks at her — she half turns away*) Answer me. (*Pause*) The Judge tells me you gave up what was yours — to me — without no other reason than because you wanted me to have it. That's true, ain't it? (*Pause*) You sent me every cent you had, when you knew mother was dying, then you went bail for me, like he said — and did all them other things. I don't know as any woman ever did any more —. I want to know why!

JANE

Why do you think?

BEN

I don't know — I sort of thought — sort of hoped ——

JANE (*bravely*)

It was because I loved her, Ben ——

BEN

Oh.

[*He turns away disappointed.*

JANE

You're forgetting, I guess, how long we was alone here — when you was in France — then the months we did n't know where you was, when the police was looking for you — She used to make me promise if ever I could I'd help you.

BEN

Well — all I 've got to say is you 're no liar.

JANE

Good-by.

[*She turns to go.*

BEN

Wait. (*Closes door*) Let 's see that letter you said she left for you.

JANE

No. I won't do that. I 've done enough; you 're free, you 've got the money and the farm.

BEN (*crosses in front of table and sits left of table*)

They ain't worth a damn with you gone — I did n't know that till just now, but they ain't.

JANE

It 's sort of sudden, the way you found that out.

BEN

Oh, it don't take long for a man to get hungry — it only takes just a minute for a man to die; you can burn down a barn quick enough, or do a murder; it 's just living and getting old that takes a lot of time — Can't you stay here, Jane?

JANE

There 's Nettie.

BEN

Nettie — that could n't stand the gaff — that run out on me when I was in trouble.

JANE

It does n't matter what folks do, if you love 'em enough.

BEN

What do you know about it? I suppose you 've been in love a lot of times?

JANE

No.

BEN

Then you be quiet and let an expert talk. I was lonesome and I wanted a woman; she was pretty and I wanted to kiss her — that ain't what I call love.

JANE

You. You don't even know the meaning of the word.

BEN

That don't worry me none — I guess the feller that wrote the dictionary was a whole lot older 'n I am before he got down to the L's.

JANE

You 've got good in you, Ben, deep down, if you 'd only try. (*Ben turns*) I know, it 's always been that way! You 've never tried for long; you 've never had a real ambition.

BEN

When I was a kid I wanted to spit farther than anybody.

JANE

Good-by.

[*She starts up to door.*

BEN

And so you 're going to break your word?

JANE (*hurt — turns*)

BEN

I don't know what 't was you promised mother, but you 've broke your word. No man ever needed a woman more 'n I need you, and you 're leaving me.

JANE

That is n't fair.

BEN

It's true, ain't it; truth ain't always fair — You ain't helped me none, you 've hurt me — worse than being broke, worse than bein' in jail.

JANE

It don't seem like I could stand to have you talk like that.

BEN

What you done you done for her. I did n't count, I never have, not with you.

JANE

When you 've been trying to do a thing as long as I have, it gets to be a part of you.

BEN

You done it all for her — well — she 's dead — you 'd better go.

JANE

Maybe I had, but if I do it will be with the truth between us. Here 's the letter she left for me, Ben — I got a feeling somehow like she was here with us now, like she wanted you to read it. (*She holds it out*) It 's like she was guiding us from the grave — Read it.

[*Crosses up to window.*

BEN (*reads*)

" My dear Jane: The doctor tells me I have n't long to live and so I am doing this, the meanest thing I think I 've ever done to you. I 'm leaving you the Jordan money. Since my husband died there has been just one person I could get to care about, that 's Ben, who was my baby so long after all the others had forgotten how to love me. (*He mumbles the letter to himself, then brings out the words*) "Hold

out her heart and let him trample on it, as he has
on mine."

[*Slowly he breaks down, sobbing bitterly.*

JANE

Don't, Ben ——

BEN

Look what I done to her.   Look what I done.

JANE (*hand on his shoulder*)

Oh, my dear — my dear!

BEN

I did love her, mor'n she thought, mor'n I ever knew
how to tell her!

JANE (*kneels beside him*)

It was n't all your fault — you were a lonely boy —
she never said much — she was like you, Ben,
ashamed to show the best that 's in you.

BEN (*bitterly*)

The best in me.   I ain't fit that you should touch me
Jane — you 'd better go.

JANE

Not if you need me, Ben, and I think you do.

BEN

I love you — mor'n I ever thought I could — ten-
derer —truer — but I 'm no good — You could n't
trust me — I could n't trust myself.

JANE

Spring's coming, Ben, everywhere, to you and me, if
you would only try.

BEN

Can a feller change — Just 'cause he wants to?

JANE

I don't want you changed. I want you what you are, the best of you — just a man that loves me — if you do love me, Ben.

BEN

Can't you help me to be fit?

JANE

I'm going to do the thing I always meant to do — Good times and bad, Ben, I'm going to share with you.

BEN

God knows I ——

JANE

Hush, Ben — I don't want another promise.

BEN

What do you want?

JANE

You said I was a good sport once — You shook hands on what we'd do to bring this old place back — there's plenty to be done. I'll stay and help you if you want me.

BEN

A good sport? (*He takes her hand*) I'll say you're all of that.

[*Hannah enters.*

HANNAH

If you ain't careful you'll miss that train.

JANE

That's just what I want to do.

HANNAH

You ain't going?

JANE

I'm never going, Hannah.

HANNAH

You going to marry him?

BEN

You bet your life she is!

HANNAH

I guess you 'll be mighty happy — marriage changes folks — and any change in him will be a big improvement.

[*She picks up Jane's bag and exits — Jane and Ben laugh.*